T0157868

Dancing for Fun

Dancing for Fun

Group Dancing for All Ages

Book One

Piano Compositions by
Mark L. Greathouse

Choreography Transcriptions by
Helena Greathouse

 iUniverse®

DANCING FOR FUN
GROUP DANCING FOR ALL AGES

Copyright © 2010, 2014 Mark L. & Helena Greathouse.

All rights reserved. No part of this book may be used or reproduced by any means, graphic, electronic, or mechanical, including photocopying, recording, taping or by any information storage retrieval system without the written permission of the publisher except in the case of brief quotations embodied in critical articles and reviews.

iUniverse books may be ordered through booksellers or by contacting:

iUniverse
1663 Liberty Drive
Bloomington, IN 47403
www.iuniverse.com
1-800-Authors (1-800-288-4677)

Because of the dynamic nature of the Internet, any web addresses or links contained in this book may have changed since publication and may no longer be valid. The views expressed in this work are solely those of the author and do not necessarily reflect the views of the publisher, and the publisher hereby disclaims any responsibility for them.

Any people depicted in stock imagery provided by Thinkstock are models, and such images are being used for illustrative purposes only.
Certain stock imagery © Thinkstock.

ISBN: 978-1-4917-4750-6 (sc)
ISBN: 978-1-4917-4751-3 (e)

Library of Congress Control Number: 2014918558

Printed in the United States of America.

iUniverse rev. date: 11/24/2014

We wish to dedicate this book to the following people:

to Mark's father, Alfred Greathouse, who gave him the gift of music, and

to Marilyn Olson, who inspired us to create this book, edited and recorded the piano score, and gave us invaluable advice throughout.

Contents

Preface

We all have the urge to move and dance to music and rhythm. We find ourselves and see others tapping their feet and moving their bodies to rhythms that touch each of us in positive ways. We may not even be aware that our bodies are moving. It's really magical, when you think about it. This book taps into the universal, primal human desire for expression in the form of dance.

If you want to dance in a group of any size, at any age, you can easily do it using this book. No experience is required. A glossary at the back of the book tells you exactly how to do a particular move.

When we prepared this book, we wanted to make sure that you could learn the dance as easily as possible and have fun at the same time. Now give it a try!

We especially wish to thank:

Angelle Hebert and Phillip Kraft. Angelle created the choreography, and Phillip greatly helped in the creation of both audio and video.

Renee Adams for her professional dancing to each composition for the instructional online video.

Elizabeth Berg for her artistic talent in creating the cover of the book.

Gail Watson for her skills in designing the book.

Jim Starr for his technical knowledge and skills and generosity in helping us with various computer hardware and software issues.

Introduction

This book was written for people of all ages who would like to dance. This includes homeschoolers all the way to seniors who live in independent living facilities. The dances can perhaps be best described as folk-inspired, contemporary dances. Each selection of music and each dance is completely original. Best of all, you can watch each dance performed by one dancer of the group. Go to our website www.greathouseofmusic.com and click the tab "Dancing for Fun, Book 1". At the back of the book, you will also find the links to YouTube to see each dance performed. The written choreography for each dance is there for reference to match the dance exactly with the music. These dances are meant to be done in a group, which just invites having a lot of fun with other dancers. The dances are not in any particular order, so just pick a dance and start learning it. Check the Glossary at the back of the book to learn the meaning of the italicized words that you'll find throughout.

Mark and Helena Greathouse are a musical duo and live in Portland, Oregon. Mark plays the accordion, and Helena sings and dances. They call themselves The Greathouse of Music. Mark's introduction to music began at the age of five when his father, a music teacher in Portland, Oregon, introduced him to the accordion. During his teenage years, Mark won several awards for his accordion performances before going to Europe to study German, where he met his future wife, Helena, from Prague.

Since age seven, Helena sang on the Czechoslovak National Radio. Throughout her childhood, Helena performed in musicals on both the Czechoslovak National TV and live theater in her native Czechoslovakia. Her dance teacher was a direct pupil of Isadora Duncan. In teenage years, Helena turned to competitive sports, competing in rhythmic gymnastics for twelve years in Europe on the advanced level. That led to pursuing an international judging career later in her life representing the United States (including three World Championships, Pan Am and Goodwill Games, and two Olympics).

Mark loves to compose melodies, especially on the piano. It turns out that they actually lend themselves quite well to dance. This combination of melody and dance has led to writing *Dancing for Fun*, books one and two. The dances have been professionally choreographed, and Helena's extensive rhythmic gymnastics background has helped immensely in capturing the exact movement in written form.

Riverflow

What better way to experience peace of mind than to float down a river at a leisurely pace in a small boat.

Riverflow

Dancing For Fun
Book 1

Moderato

Mark L. Greathouse

Riverflow Choreography

Key Signature: 2/4

Introduction: 8 measures

Measures 1–8: Start in circle holding hands, facing the center of the circle. Spread out to begin allowing space for arms to stretch downward. Hold formation for first phrase of music (8 measures) as an introduction.

Measures 9–12: Start on right foot. Walk 4 steps into the center of the circle (1 measure = 2 counts), slowly raising straight arms up. Then reverse. Walk back from the center, lowering straight arms slowly down. Movement of head always follows arm movement.

Measures 13–16: Repeat movement of measures 9–12.

Measures 17–20: *Step together* to the right 4 times (each step on 2 counts). Continue to hold hands.

Measures 21–24: *Step together* to the left 4 times (each step on 2 counts). Continue to hold hands.

Measures 25–26: Step forward with the right, then close left leg to right leg, swing straight arms up. Then step back with the left, close right leg to left leg, swing straight arms down.

Measures 27–28: Repeat movement of measures 25–26.

Measures 29–32: Release hands and circle the arms in frontal plane down and up (*arm sequence*). Each person walking individually around his/her own circle in place, circling to the right.

Measures 33–48: Repeat whole dance with modifications.

♫ Measures 33–36: Repeat movement of measures 9–12.

♫ Measures 37–38: *Step together* to the right twice (each step on 2 counts), continue to hold hands.

♫ Measures 39–40: Same as measures 37–38 but to the left.

♫ Measures 41–44: Repeat movement of measures 25–26 twice.

♫ Measures 45–48: Repeat movement of measures 29–32.

Measures 49–50: Stand still, legs together, arms down at sides.

Spring Rain

April showers do bring
May flowers. Sometimes
the showers grow into
deafening thunderstorms.

Spring Rain

Dancing for Fun
Book 1

Spring Rain Choreography

Key Signature: 4/4

Introduction: 4 measures

Measures 1–4: Start in small circle holding hands, facing the center of the circle. Spread out to allow space for arms to stretch. Hold formation for first phrase of music (4 measures) as an introduction.

Measures 5–8: Turn 90 degrees to right so that left side of body faces center of circle when starting movement. Stepping on right, skip on right. Continue skipping in a circle alternating legs, holding hands for 8 skips, each skip on 2 counts.

Measures 9–12: release hands and do 2 *hops with wiggles*.

♫ Measures 9–10: With change of music theme, hop-turning 180 degrees to right, landing in *second position*, facing out from circle and wiggle arms.

♫ Measures 11–12: Hop-turning 180 degrees to right again, landing in *second position*, facing center of circle and wiggle arms.

Measures 13–16: Same as movement of measures 5–8 but to left.

Section A. (Containing A1 and A2)

A1. Measures 17–20:

♫ Measures 17–18: With change of music theme, face center of circle, hold hands again, and do 2 *gallops* to right, each *gallop* on 2 counts. Then *step together* to the right and clap on last count.

♫ Measures 19–20: Same as movement of measures 17–18 but to the left.

A2. Measures 21–24:

♫ Measures 21–22: Release hands and do 3 *chaines* to right (each *chaines* on 1 count) around the perimeter of the circle, and clap on last count.

♫ Measures 23–24: Same as movement of measures 21–22 but to the left.

Measures 25–32: Repeat movement of Section A.

Section B. (Containing B1 and B2) (in music repeat measures 17–24)

B1. Measures 33–36: Modified movement of A1.

Modification: Add a kick at the end of each gallop series, kicking the leg opposite to the direction of galloping. Kick is in frontal plane inward, kicking leg nearly touching the supporting leg.

B2. Measures 37–40: Modified movement of A2.

Modification: Add *arm sequence* with *chaines*. Add kick in frontal plane across the body (described in B1) during clap.

Measures 25–31 (in music plus measure 41): Repeat movement of Section B.

Measures 1–8 (in music): Repeat movement of measures 5–8 twice.

Measures 9–12 (in music): Repeat movement of measures 9–12.

Measures 13–16 (in music): Repeat movement of measures 5–8 but to left.

Just Gettin' By

Are some of our brothers and sisters struggling in life just to survive? I know some people just gettin' by. Do you? What are you doing about it?

Just Gettin' By

Dancing for Fun
Book 1

Mark L. Greathouse

Playfully

Piano

Just Gettin' By Choreography

Key Signature: 4/4

Introduction: 1 measure

Measure 1: Start in 2 lines facing each other, with lines of dancers 90 degrees to audience.

Measure 2: With hands on hips (alternatively arms down at sides), walk 3 steps forward toward partner (1 step per count), starting with right and hop on right on last count.

Measure 3: With hands on hips (alternatively arms down at sides), walk 3 steps back away from partner (1 step per count), starting with left and hop on left on last count.

Measures 4-5: Repeat movement of measures 2-3.

Measure 6: Starting with right, walk 3 steps toward partner and *step together* right forward on the fourth count. Gradually raise arms sideways up in frontal plane, and on the fourth count, touch your partner's palms, arms raised, elbows bent, fingers spread.

Measures 7-8: Maintaining contact with partner's palms, do *step together* 2 times toward audience and reverse direction doing *step together* 2 times away from audience.

Measure 9: Releasing contact with partner, walk 3 steps away from your partner, starting with left, and *step together* left, backward on the fourth count. Gradually lower arms sideways in frontal plane, and on the fourth count put arms on hips.

Measures 10-17: Repeat movement of measures 2-9 from the beginning.

Measures 18-19: 4 *pivot steps* on the right, hands on hips (alternatively arms down at sides).

Measure 20: Walk 4 steps forward toward partner, starting with right, arms down at sides.

Measures 21-22: Partners touch right palms and walk around in small circle to the right.

Measures 23-24: Change direction of hands, and repeat movement of measures 21-22 to the left.

Measure 25: Return to original two lines, walking backward 4 steps while putting hands back on hips (alternatively arms down at sides).

Measures 18-25 in music, repeat movement of measures 18-25 to opposite direction.

Measures 26-33 in music, repeat movement of measures 2-9 from the beginning of the dance.

Measures 34-42 in music, repeat movement of measures 2-9 from the beginning of the dance.

Soul Song

Listen to your voice within, and let it inspire you to become your true potential.

Soul Song

Dancing for Fun
Book 1

Mark L. Greathouse

Soul Song Choreography

Key Signature: 2/4

Introduction: 8 measures.

Measures 1–8: Remain in place. Stand in circle, holding hands facing outward from the center of the circle. Spread out to allow space for arms to stretch. After 2 measures of music, start arm movements: arms snaking on sides, elbows leading movement up and down, alternating arms.

A. Measures 9–16: Arms snaking on sides, elbows leading movement up and down, alternating arms while doing *step together* 4 times to right side (2 measures each step) and staying connected.

B. Measures 17–24: Assign each dancer a number between one and four. Release hands, turn 90 degrees to right so that right shoulder of each dancer is toward center of circle. Do a total of 4 *windmill arms* to right (2 measures each windmill). Dancers perform this movement in a *canon* toward the center of circle; each dancer in succession performs one *windmill arms* and holds still when it is not his/her turn to move. Finish in *demi plie*, legs together.

C. Measures 9–16 (in music): Turn 90 degrees to right so that each dancer faces the center of circle. Holding hands, repeat A, moving to right.

D. Measures 17–24 (in music): Turn 90 degrees to right and do a total of 4 *windmill arms* to right in *canon* away from center of the circle (see B).

E. Measures 25–32: Turn 90 degrees to right to face outward from the center of the circle. Movement is done around large circle.

♫ Measure 25: Slide right leg to the right along floor into *second position demi plie*, keep torso upright while stretching and gradually raising arms to the front high diagonal, shaking the hands, palms flexed.

♫ Measure 26: Keep shaking hands while lowering the arms close to the body, straightening legs and closing left leg to right leg in toe stand.

♫ Measures 27–28: Repeat measures 25–26, traveling to right.

♫ Measures 29–32: Movement as in measures 25–28 but to opposite side (traveling to left).

F. Measures 33–40: Turn 90 degrees to right so that right shoulder of each dancer is toward center of circle. Movement is done around large circle.

♪ Measures 33–34: In one action right *lunge* forward, head and torso leaning forward, back straight, in one line with left leg, which is stretched backward, toes touching floor. With left elbow leading, stretch left arm through *develope* in a half circle from behind the body to reach position in line with the torso and the left leg.

♪ Measures 35–36: As measures 33–34, but left *lunge* and *develope* with right arm.

♪ Measures 37–40: Repeat measures 33–36.

G. Measures 41–56:

♪ Measures 41–48: Turn 90 degrees to right to face center of circle. Take 4 long steps backward (2 measures for each step), starting on right and alternating legs while doing **one** slow reverse *arm sequence* (for duration of these measures).

♪ Measures 49–56: Take 4 long steps forward (2 measures for each step) as follows: Turning out right leg, step right on the diagonal forward in *demi plie* and subsequently straighten right knee. Keep weight on right, left toes touching the floor behind the body. Rotating torso to right, impulse forward in left shoulder. Left arm follows the impulse until crossing in front of the body in horizontal plane. Right arm ends up low and behind the body at the end of rotation, elbow slightly bent. Head moves to right. Repeat 4 times alternating legs (right, left, right, left). Eight measures total, 2 measures per movement, or as an option (in video) repeat movement of F (above) moving toward center of circle.

H. Measures 57–72 (and again 57–72 in music): Repeat A., B., C., and D., but start doing *step together*, facing into the circle with *windmill arms* moving into the circle, followed by *step together* facing out from the circle with *windmill arms* moving out from the circle.

I. Measures 73–82: As a *canon*, turn 90 degrees to left, and crossing right arm low and close in front of body, reach right arm outward from circle, and move right arm in *frontal plane* up and overhead to center of circle. Quickly meet the other dancers' hands, touching in the center of the circle. Then each dancer stretches right arm as high as possible, shaking the hand. On the last note of the music, everyone falls away from the center of the circle to the ground.

Rainbow

The symbol of God's promise is one of the gems of nature.
When you see one, you are witnessing one of nature's jewels.

Rainbow

Dancing for Fun
Book 1

Gently

Mark L. Greathouse

Rainbow Choreography

Key Signature: 4/4

Introduction: 1 measure (not in music)

Start in a big circle, facing center of circle. Allow introduction to go by without movement. Arms are down at the sides of body.

Section A:

Measure 1: *Grapevine step* to right, arms to sides.

Measure 2:

♫ Counts 1 and 2: *Step hop* on right with left leg in *passé* position. Clap hands in front of body during the hop on second count.

♫ Counts 3 and 4: With arms to sides, *chaines* turn to left to finish facing center of circle

Measures 3-4: Repeat measures 1 and 2 to opposite side.

Measure 5: *Rainbow step* to right.

Measure 6: *Rainbow step* to left.

Measure 7: Turn 90 degrees to left, and place right toes into center of circle while standing on left. Shift weight onto right leg, and spin on right leg with *side body wave* in torso with *windmill arms* to right, finishing to face outward of circle (turn 180 degrees to right). Left leg is in low *arabesque*.

Measure 8: Repeat measure 7 to opposite side with initial step outside of circle, finishing facing center of the circle.

Measures 9-16: Repeat measures 1-8.

Section B:

Measure 17: *Balance step* forward on right.

Measure 18: *Balance step* forward on left.

Measure 19:

♫ Counts 1-2: Facing center of circle, step right side into *second position demi plie*, *presentational arms*.

♫ Counts 3-4: Straighten right leg, turning 180 degrees to right on flat foot into *second position demi plie*, maintaining *presentational arms* (*chaines*).

Measure 20:

♪ Counts 1-2: Straightening left leg, turn 180 degrees to right on flat foot into *second position demi plie*, close arms to hips (*chaines*).

♪ Counts 3-4: Straighten knees and close left leg to right, keeping hands on hips.

Measures 21-24: Repeat Section B to opposite side.

Measures 25-28: Repeat Section B (in original direction), replacing steps with hops on each *balance step* and each *chaines*. (Each *demi plie* is followed by a hop.)

Measures 29-46: Repeat Section A.

Measure 47: *Demi plie*, legs together, head down, dorsal bend forward, head down.

Measure 48: Gradually straighten body, starting with trunk. Head finishes movement into straight stand, arms down at sides, legs together.

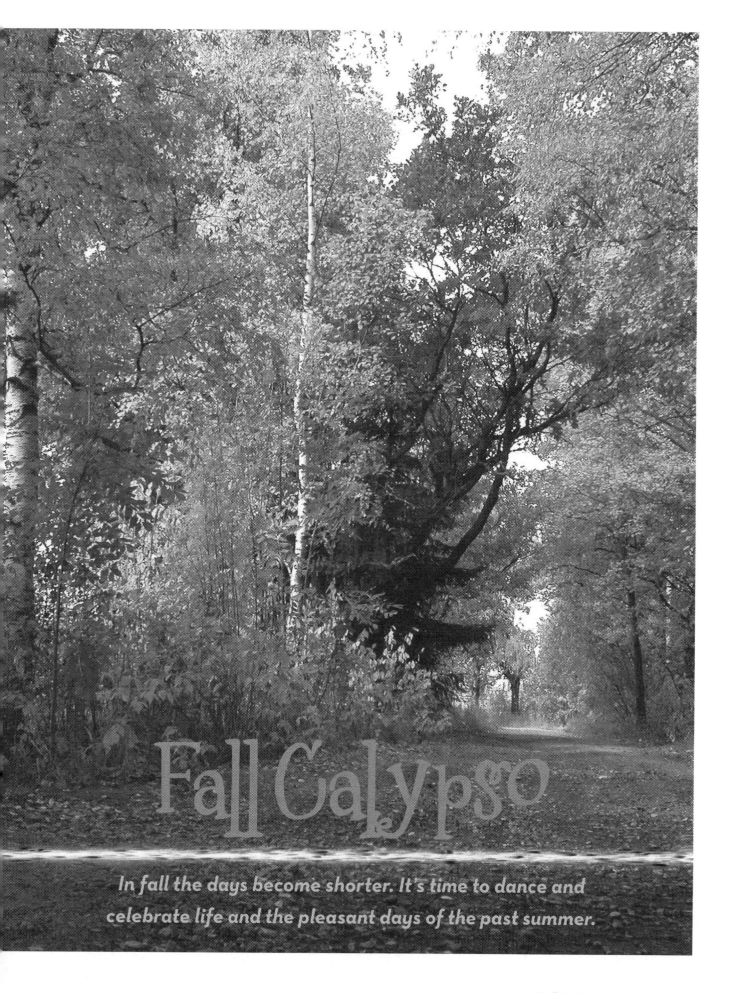

Fall Calypso

In fall the days become shorter. It's time to dance and celebrate life and the pleasant days of the past summer.

Fall Calypso

Dancing For Fun
Book 1

Mark L. Greathouse

Lightly

Fall Calypso Choreography

Key Signature: 4/4

Introduction: 3 chords (not in music)

Start in 2 staggered lines facing front, dancers arm-length apart from each other, arms are down at the sides of body, allow introduction to go by without movement.

Section A:

Measure 1:

♫ Count 1: Step forward diagonally on right heel, *presentational arms*.

♫ Count 2: Step forward diagonally on left heel, maintain *presentational arms*.

♫ Count 3: Step back right on toes, keeping feet same distance apart, putting hands on hips.

♫ Count 4: Step back left on toes, maintain hands on hips, keep feet same distance apart.

Measures 2-4: Repeat movement of measure 1 three times.

Measure 5:

♫ Counts 1-2: Cross right foot in front, turn 90 degrees left, right *demi plie*, shifting weight to right. Arms *port de bra* from *first position*, head slightly down, *dorsal bend* forward.

♫ Counts 3-4: Jump on right, turning 180 degrees to right, left leg in low back *attitude* (bent leg behind). Arms open to low diagonal, head looking over left shoulder, *dorsal bend* backward.

Measures 6-8: Repeat movement of measure 5 three times, alternating sides.

Measures 9-16: Repeat Section A.

Measure 17:

♫ Counts 1-3: With *arms first position*, *chaines* turns forward to right (step right, left, right) finishing in *demi plie* on right.

♫ Count 4: Hold in *demi plie* on right.

Measure 18: With arms down by sides, hop back 4 times, alternating feet (left, right, left, right), finishing with left leg up forward low.

Measures 19-20: Repeat movement of measures 17-18 to opposite side.

Measures 21-24: Repeat movement of measures 17-20.

Measure 25: Coda Step:

♫ Counts 1-2: Reach backward on diagonal with right foot, and shift weight onto the right into *demi plie*, *dorsal bend* backward, arms raised to V, palms facing out. Left leg is in front in *attitude*.

♫ Counts 3-4: Step forward left into *demi plie*, bending right leg behind left leg, right toes touching floor, arms down at sides of body, head slightly down, *dorsal bend* forward.

Measure 26:

♫ Count 1: Turning 135 degrees to right, step on right, arms down at sides of body.

♫ Count 2: Balance on right with left leg in parallel front *attitude*, keeping arms down.

♫ Count 3: Hold shape of legs and clap in front.

♫ Count 4: Hold whole shape of arms and legs and turn head to look over left shoulder.

Measure 27:

♫ Counts 1-2: Step left side with left *side body wave*, keeping weight on left leg, bend right leg beside left leg, right toes touching floor, arms down at sides of body.

♫ Counts 3-4: Repeat counts 1-2 to opposite side.

Measures 28-29: Turning 180 degrees to left, repeat measures 26-27 to opposite side.

Measures 30-33: Repeat measures 26-29, moving upstage (away from audience).

Measure 34: Turn to face forward toward audience, legs together, arms down.

Measures 35-50: Repeat movement of Section A twice.

Measure 51: Repeat movement of measure 25.

Mourek Saunter

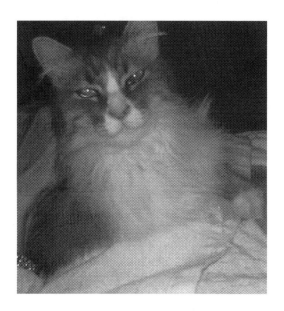

Mourek is one of our kitties with a Czech name. She is a bit heavy and sometimes slow on her feet—therefore, she saunters. Take a look at her. She is beautiful.

Mourek Saunter

Dancing for Fun
Book 1

Lazily ♩ = 66

Piano

Mark L. Greathouse

Mourek Saunter Choreography

Key Signature: 2/4

No introduction; dance begins on first count.

Start in 2 lines facing each other, with lines of dancers 90 degrees to audience.

Section A

Measure 1: Step on right foot on a diagonal, lift bent left leg keeping thigh parallel with floor. Angle of left bent knee is slightly more than 90 degrees, left foot flexed; remain standing on right, and rotate left hip in about 30 degrees; arms are "runner" style with hands in fists and elbows bent, arms move in opposite direction than legs. In measure 1 right arm is in front over left leg; left arm is behind body. During rotation the torso rotates in opposite direction than hip; in measure 1 torso rotates to left. Dancers move forward toward the other line of dancers. (Torso rotation is optional, as in the video.)

Measure 2: Repeat measure 1 but start with left foot and transpose movement accordingly.

Measures 3 and 4: Repeat measures 1 and 2.

Measures 5-8: 4 *Heel drags backward* (right, left, right, left), lines of dancers moving backward away from each other.

Measures 9-12: Repeat measure 1-4 but without body rotation, moving straight forward (right, left, right, left).

Measures 13-16: Maintaining left leg in the same place during these measures, step with right forward, shifting weight to right leg in the beginning of each measure; then turn 90 degrees to left, shifting weight to left leg. With each step and turn (corresponding to one measure in music), the hips rock in the direction of shifted weight. With elbows bent and close to the body, the wrists bend in and out (flick out with the right step and in with the left turn). In the fourth measure, end with feet together and arms down by the sides (lines of dancers end up facing each other).

Measures 1-12 followed by 17-20 (in music): Repeat Section A starting on left foot.

Section B

Measure 21: Turn 90 degrees to left (half of dancers face audience, other half with back to audience); step with right foot to right side, dragging left toes on floor while looking over left shoulder, hands in fists are placed on hips.

Measure 22: Step again with right foot to right side, dragging left toes on floor while looking over left shoulder, hands in fists are placed on hips. End with feet together at end of this measure.

Measures 23-24: Turn 180 degrees to right, and repeat Measures 21 and 22 to the left.

Measure 25: *Chaines* turn 360 degrees to right with hands in fists on hips.

Measure 26: Turn additional 90 degrees to right to face other line of dancers, ending up with legs together in parallel *demi plie*; slap both hands on thighs on the last count.

Measures 27-28: Repeat 4 *heel drags backwards* (right, left, right, left), from Section A, but twice as fast, lines of dancers moving backward away from each other. When stepping back, the wrists flex outward and immediately come back in (flicking with each step). Keep looking forward.

Measures 29-36: Repeat Section B to opposite side, starting with left.

Measures 21-32 and 37-40: Repeat all of Section A to opposite side, starting with left.

Measures 41-48: Repeat all of Section A as written. Movement described in measures 13-16.

Measures 49-52: Repeat movement of measures 1-4.

Measures 53-55: Repeat movement of measures 13-16.

Measure 56: Step right forward toward other line of dancers, and then step left forward and lift right leg back with knee bent in *back attitude* with "runner" arms and hold on straight standing left leg to finish (ending in *back attitude* balance).

Macek Rag

Macek is our other kitty. She is smart although her name in Czech implies heaviness. She is not that, as you can see.

Macek Rag

Dancing for Fun
Book 1

Macek Rag Choreography

Key Signature: 2/4

Introduction: 1 measure

Measure 1: Introduction. Remain in place. Start in 2 lines facing each other, dancers with side to audience. During the introduction, stand still with arms closed at sides, feet together.

Section A:

Measure 2: Moving forward toward the other line of dancers, slide right toes on floor in arc shape toward front, then to the side, and shift weight onto right foot. As right foot moves, right arm moves simultaneously in horizontal plane, arm is rotated in, so palm is facing out. Arm follows the pattern of the foot.

Measure 3: Continuing to move forward toward the other line of dancers, repeat measure 1 to opposite side.

Measures 4–5: Reversing the direction of movement, repeat measure 1 now moving backward. Legs move back, side and close and arms move back, side and in and are turned in.

Measure 6:

♫ Count 1: Step forward right into *demi plie* allowing torso to fall forward, bending at the waist, head down, and arms slightly bent at elbows and lifted slightly back in *sagittal plane*, palms facing forward. Left leg bent, shin less than horizontal, left toes pointed but not quite touching floor. Knees and thighs of both legs together.

♫ Count 2: Step back left, lifting right leg in front in *parallel attitude*, keeping the shape of arms, lift arms forward high, looking up at hands.

Measure 7:

♫ Count 1: Step forward right, releasing the arms down to sides of body.

♫ Count 2: Step forward left into *demi plie*, allowing torso to fall forward, bending at the waist, head down, and arms slightly bent at elbows and lifted slightly back in *sagittal plane*, palms facing forward. Right leg bent, shin less than horizontal, right toes pointed but not quite touching floor. Knees and thighs of both legs together.

Measure 8:

♫ Count 1: Step back right, lifting left leg in front in *parallel attitude*, keeping the shape of arms, lift arms forward high, looking up at hands.

♫ Count 2: Step back left.

Measure 9: Step back right, and then close left to right to end with feet together. During these steps, arms open to sides and finally close to body.

Measures 10-17: Repeat Section A to the opposite side.

Measures 18-33: Repeat Section A twice, first to right then to left.

Section B

Measures 34-35: Four *prancing* steps moving forward, starting with right and alternating legs.

Measures 36-37: Four *prancing* steps moving backward, starting with right and alternating legs.

Measure 38: Stepping front right, swing left leg forward in, crossing in front of body, in turned out front *attitude*, knee leading the movement, knee of right (support) leg remains straight. As left leg swings forward in, arms drop down and swing in *frontal plane*, crossing in front of body at waist level.

Measure 39: Swing left leg back in, turned out *attitude*, while the arms swing downward in *frontal plane* and open to the sides horizontal. Right (support) leg remains straight.

Measure 40: While continuing to balance on right (support) straight leg, swing left leg forward in, crossing in front of body, in turned out front *attitude*, knee leading the movement and open around to the side in turned outside *attitude* in a circular pattern. As left leg swings forward in, arms drop down and swing in *frontal plane*, crossing in front of body at waist level, then with swing in frontal plane open to sides.

Measure 41: While continuing swinging movement, lower left leg behind right leg, and then close left to right. Arms remain side horizontal.

Measures 42-49: Repeat Section B to opposite side.

Measures 2-17 (in music): Repeat Section B twice, first to right, and then to left.

Measures 18-33 (in music): Repeat Section A twice, first to right, and then to left.

Measures 34-45 (in music) followed by 50-53: Repeat Section A twice again, first to right, and then to left.

Awakening

Just as we awaken to
a new day, so we may
awaken anytime to a
new dimension or a new
direction in our life.

Awakening

Dancing for Fun
Book 1

Lento

Mark L. Greathouse

Awakening Choreography

Key Signature: 3/4

Introduction: 4 measures

Measures 1-4: Introduction. Start in a big circle facing center of circle, allowing introduction to go by without movement.

Section A

During this section arms are down at sides of body.

During measures 5-8 movement is done around the circumference of big circle.

Measure 5: *Waltz step* (right down, left up, right up) to right starting with right leg, head turns to right on first count. Turn 180 degrees to right during this measure to face outside of circle.

Measure 6: *Waltz step* (left down, right up, left up) to right starting with left leg, head turns to left on first count. Turn 180 degrees to right to face center of circle.

Measures 7-8: Repeat measures 5 and 6; end facing center of circle.

Measure 9: Walk toward center of circle starting with right, and then step left, then right, and *demi plie* on right, with left leg bent behind right, left toes touching floor.

Measure 10: Walk backward from center of circle starting with left, and then step back right, step back left, and *demi plie* on left with right leg bent in front, right toes touching floor.

Measure 11: *Pas de basque* to right.

Measure 12: *Pas de basque* to left.

Measures 13-20: Repeat Section A.

Section B

During this section, arms are down at sides of body. Before starting movement, turn 90 degrees to left, so that right shoulder is toward center of circle.

Measures 21-22: 2 *grapevine steps* to right, ending with feet together and clapping on count 6.

Measures 23-24: Repeat measure 21-22 to left, moving away from center of circle.

During measures 25-28 movement is done around the circumference of big circle.

Measure 25: *Chasse* step on right and step right, turning 180 degrees to right.

Measure 26: Step left backward, step right backward, and close left to right.

Measures 27-28: Repeat measures 25-26.

Measures 29-36: Repeat Section B on opposite side, starting with left.

Measures 37-52: Repeat Section A twice on opposite side, each time starting with left.

Stepping Along

Life is moving along. Try something new, take a risk, and follow the opportunities that come your way. Stay out of the rocking chair.

Stepping Along

Dancing for Fun
Book 1

Andante

♩ = 108

Mark L. Greathouse

Piano

Stepping Along Choreography

Key Signature: 4/4

Introduction: 8 measures

Measures 1–8: Introduction. Start in a circle holding hands facing center of circle. During the introduction, stand still.

Section A (Measures 1–8 of this section use music measures 1–8.)

Measure 1:

♪ Counts 1–2: Turn 90 degrees to right, still holding hands, and *step together* with right front.

♪ Counts 3–4: Step right front.

Measure 2:

♪ Counts 1–2: Still holding hands, *step together* with left front.

♪ Counts 3–4: Step left front.

Measure 3: Turn 90 degrees to left to face center of circle, and do modified *grapevine step* to right (step right, cross behind, step right, cross front).

Measure 4: Stepping forward right to the center of the circle, do half of *pivot step* on right (step right, turn 180 degrees left to face out of the circle, shifting weight to left). During the turn, release the hands and grab them again at the end of the turn.

Measures 5–8: Repeat movement of preceding measures 1–4, now facing out of the circle. Movement is done to the right again.

Measures 9–16 in music: Repeat Section A (again facing in and then facing out).

Section B

Measure 17:

♪ Counts 1–3: Three *chaine* steps (right front, left with turn of 180 degrees to right, right back) moving toward center of circle, to finish facing out of circle. Hands on hips.

♪ Count 4: *Demi plie* on right with left leg stretched forward, heel touching floor, foot flexed, and torso leaning forward slightly.

Measure 18: Repeat measure 17 in opposite direction (turning to left, finish facing into circle).

Measure 19: Stepping on right, lift left leg in front *parallel attitude*, continue circular movement of left leg, knee leading from front to side in arc, finish lowering left leg to floor so that final stand is in *second position*.

Measure 20: Repeat measure 19 in opposite direction.

Measures 21–24: Repeat measures 17–20.

Measures 17–24 in music: Repeat Section B sequence.

Section C (Hands on hips throughout measures 25 and 26.)

Measure 25:

♫ Counts 1–2: Turning 90 degrees to right so that left shoulder is facing center of circle, *step together* with right front.

♫ Counts 3–4: Step right front.

Measure 26:

♫ Counts 1–2: *Step together* with left front.

♫ Counts 3–4: Step left front.

Measure 27:

♫ Count 1: Turning 90 degrees to left to face center of circle, step on right in *demi plie* and lift left leg in turned out front *attitude*.

♫ Count 2: Standing on right, hit inside of left ankle with right hand.

♫ Count 3: Continuing to stand on right, rotate left leg inward, and hit the outside of left ankle with left hand.

♫ Count 4: Finish lowering left leg to floor so that final stand is in *second position*.

Measure 28: Stepping left front, repeat measure 27 (ankle slaps) to the opposite side.

Measures 29–32: Repeat movement of preceding measures 25-28 in opposite direction to left, starting with right shoulder toward center of circle.

Measures 33–40: Repeat Section C.

Section D

Measure 41:

♫ Counts 1–2: Turning 90 degrees to right with left shoulder into center of circle, put hands on the shoulders of dancer in front of you. Extending right leg straight low front, foot flexed, *chasse* on right forward.

♫ Counts 3–4: Repeat right *chasse* with flexed foot.

Measure 42:

♫ Counts 1–2: Repeat right *chasse* with flexed foot.

♫ Counts 3-4: Step forward left and hop on left with right leg bent in low *passe* with right foot touching left ankle.

Measure 43: Repeat measure 41 without initial turn.

Measure 44:

♫ Counts 1-2: Repeat right *chasse* with flexed foot.

♫ Counts 3-4: Step forward left and do half of *pivot step* on left (step left, turn 180 degrees right to be with right shoulder into center of circle). Release hands from the shoulders during the turn, and put them on the other neighbor's shoulders at the end of the turn.

Measures 45-48: Movement of preceding measures 41-44 to opposite direction. (Repeat to left, starting with right shoulder toward center of circle.)

Measures 49-56: Repeat Section D.

Waltz in Eb

Doesn't the waltz invite you to dance? Three dans par disgottes mes surge ... *flo ...*
that all good things come in threes.

Waltz in Eb

Dancing for Fun
Book 1

Mark L. Greathouse

Tempo de Valse

Waltz in Eb Choreography

Key Signature: 3/4

Introduction: 9 measures

Measures 1-9: Introduction. Remain in place. Start in two lines facing each other about three feet apart with lines of dancers 90 degrees to audience. During the introduction, stand still.

Section A

Measures 10-17: Starting to right, do 8 *balance steps* while turning around your partner and alternating feet. Torso twists toward the leading foot. Arms are straight next to the body, palms facing forward, fingers spread. After 8 *balance steps*, complete a full circle.

Measures 18-25: Facing your partner and staying in place, do 8 *balance steps* starting on right and alternating feet with torso twisting toward the leading foot. Opposite arm than leg is forward high and turned upward, head raised facing lifted arm, while other arm is turned down and low behind body. Both elbows are slightly bent. Partners should touch wrists of lifted arms.

Measures 26-27: Stepping back on right through slight *demi plie* and immediately straightening right knee again, drag left pointed foot on the floor toward body, while scooping back, up, and front with right arm moving in *sagittal plane*. Head follows movement of arm.

Measures 28-29: Repeat measures 26-27 to opposite side, still moving backward.

Measures 30-31: Step forward on right, and repeat measures 26-27 in reverse direction, moving forward.

Measures 32-33: Repeat measures 30-31 to opposite side, still moving forward.

Measures 2-9 in music: Repeat movement of measures 10-17 in opposite direction (starting on left and circling to left).

Measures 10-29 and 34-37 in music: Repeat section A.

Section B

Measure 38: Stepping on right through demi plie, straighten right leg and twist torso to right. Left arm (opposite arm than leading leg) is forward high with palm turned upward while right arm is low behind body with palm turned down. Left leg, with toes on floor, is bent behind right leg.

Measure 39: Step back on left in *demi plie* while crossing right arm, palm up, in front of body, bending torso down slightly, head down. Left arm is straight and to side. Right leg, with toes on floor, is bent in front of left leg.

Measures 40–41: Stepping on right, do 360-degree *rainbow turn* on right leg. Finish facing your partner.

Measures 42–45: Repeat measures 38–41 to opposite side.

Measures 46–53: Repeat Section B.

Measures 38–51 and 54–55 in music: Repeat movement of measures 38–53, but do a hop instead of each step, including a hop on each turn.

Measures 56–63: Repeat movements of measures 10–17 in opposite direction (starting on left and circling to left).

Measures 64–87: Repeat Section A.

Scrambling

Schedules to meet, deadlines to make? Don't we all sometimes find ourselves scrambling to stay afloat?

Scrambling

Dancing for Fun
Book 1

Mark L. Greathouse

Scrambling Choreography

Key Signature: 4/4

Introduction: 4 measures

Measures 1-4 Introduction.

      Measures 1-2: Remain in place. Start in two staggered lines facing front, dancers arms' length apart from each other. Stand straight, arms down at sides.

      Measures 3-4: Slowly get into beginning shape with knees bent, feet parallel and slightly apart, elbows bent, palms down, and forearms parallel to the floor, focus forward.

Section A:

Measures 5-6: The Twist: Toes leading right and heels pointing left, switch alternating 4 times and moving in a straight line to right. Arms (elbows bent and palms facing down), move in opposition to the feet left and right.

Measure 7:

♬ Counts 1-2: *Develope* kick right leg side low and *explode arms* reaching above head in a V shape, *support leg* (left) straight, look up at hands.

♬ Counts 3-4: Bring everything into *parallel demi plie, dorsal bend* forward, head down.

Measure 8: Repeat measure 7 in opposite direction.

Measures 9-12: Repeat Section A in opposite direction.

Section B

Measure 13:

♬ Counts 1-2: Right leg extends diagonally forward right, right foot flexed, right heel touches floor, left hand behind head, and right hand on right hip.

♬ Counts 3-4: Taking off from left, do small hop, and repeat counts 1-2 in opposite direction putting left heel out.

Measure 14:

♬ Counts 1-2: Taking off from right, do small hop, and repeat counts 1-2 from measure 13, putting right heel out.

♫ Count 3: Slap right ball of foot on floor, and through a sliding movement backward on floor, kick right foot back. Shin is parallel to the floor, hold arms in same position as in counts 1–2.

♫ Count 4: Holding right leg in place, hop on left leg and end with feet together, arms down by sides.

Measure 15:

♫ Counts 1–2: Hop on right to right side, left leg in *parallel passe* front, *airplane arms*, torso tilted to right (direction of hopping foot).

♫ Counts 3–4: Turning 180 degrees to right and *spotting* in direction of turn, repeat counts 1–2 to opposite side (left).

Measure 16:

♫ Counts 1–2: Turning 180 degrees to right and *spotting* in direction of turn, repeat counts 1–2 to original side (right).

♫ Counts 3–4: Finish in *parallel demi plie*, legs slightly apart, arms at sides.

Measures 1–4 (in music): Repeat Section B in opposite direction. Hops.

Measures 5–8 (in music): Repeat Section A to right. Twist and kick.

Measures 9–12 (in music): Repeat Section A to left. Twist and kick.

Measures 13–16 (in music): Repeat Section B to right. Hops.

Measures 17–20 (in music): Repeat Section B to left. Hops.

Section C

Measures 21–24: Kicking the feet up backward, keeping thighs in vertical, knees together with pointed toes, run starting on right to right in each dancer's own circle for 16 counts, each running step equal to 1 count. Hands remain on hips.

Note: In measures 25 through 28, arms are moving at the same pace as the legs.

Measure 25:

♫ Count 1: Putting the weight on right heel with straight leg, reach the right arm up in a V with palms facing front and fingers spread.

♫ Count 2: Repeat count 1 to opposite side (left). At end of count 2, the V shape of arms is completed.

♫ Count 3: From the V, first collapse right side.

♫ Count 4: Collapse left side. At end of count 4, *parallel demi plie* is completed with legs together and elbows bent in sharp angle touching hips in front, hands are in fists.

Measures 26–28: Repeat measure 25 three more times.

Measures 29–32: Repeat measures 21–24 to the left.

Section D

Measure 33: Step forward right, and touch floor with left toes behind right foot while torso twists slightly to left and bends slightly to right side. Snap fingers when back foot touches floor. Elbows, close to sides of body, are bent to sides in sharp angle.

Measure 34: Step back on left, and touch floor with right toes in front snapping fingers on the touch. Torso twist and arm shape remain while torso bends slightly to left side.

Measures 35-36: Repeat measures 33-34.

Measures 37-38:

♫ Counts 1-6 (1½ measures): Three *chene* steps forward to right (while *spotting*), each step on 2 counts. Elbows, close to sides of body, are bent to sides in sharp angle.

♫ Counts 7-8 (last 2 counts of measure 38): Finish *chene* sequence by shifting weight onto right leg in *demi plie*, left toes touching floor behind right foot, and snap fingers. Torso twists slightly to left, and bends slightly to right side.

Measure 39-40:

♫ Counts 1-6 (1½ measures): Three *chene* steps moving backward to left (while *spotting*), each step on 2 counts. Elbows, close to sides of body, are bent to sides in sharp angle.

♫ Counts 7-8 (last 2 counts of measure 40): Finish *chene* sequence by shifting weight onto left leg in *demi plie*, right toes touching floor in front of left leg, and snap fingers. Torso twists slightly to left and bends slightly to left side.

Measures 41-48: Repeat Section D in opposite direction.

Measures 49-52: Repeat Section A.

Measures 53-56: Repeat Section A in opposite direction.

Measures 57-60: Repeat Section B.

Measures 61-64: Repeat Section B in opposite direction.

Glossary

Airplane arms: Arms straight out to the side in one line, palms facing down, tilt the torso sideways, keeping arms straight.

Arabesque: The position of the body supported on one leg, with the other leg extended behind the body, both knees straight, torso vertical.

Arm sequence: Circle arms in frontal plane close to front of body. Start movement by lowering arms sideways toward torso. Cross arms low in front nearly touching torso, and continue movement upward in frontal plane until hands overhead, palms facing down, look upward toward palms. Continue movement downward in frontal plane, arms opening to sides, palms up until reaching horizontal, palms turn down and continue movement downward in frontal plane until closing arms to torso on sides.

Arms *port de bra*: In ballet terms, it is a movement of the arms through different positions.

Attitude: A position in which the dancer stands (or jumps) on one leg (known as the supporting leg) while the other leg (working leg) is lifted and well turned out with the knee bent at approximately 90-degree angle. The lifted, or working, leg can be behind (*derrière*), in front (*devant*), or on the side (*à la seconde*) of the body.

Balance step forward on right: Rock step crossing right foot in front of left. Lift left foot behind with *demi plie* on right, and then step back on left and finish feet together. *Presentational arms* on cross step, and then move arms to hips on back step.

Canon: Dancers perform the same movement in succession, one dancer after the other (each dancer on an assigned beat in the music).

Chaines: A series of turns (each 180 degrees) as if in a "chain," alternating feet with progression along a straight line or circle. Head spotting. Usually done in very small steps with straight knees, all steps on toes; can also be executed on flat feet or in *demi plie*.

Chasse step on right: A sliding step in which one foot "chases" and displaces the other. It is a traveling step. Literally "to chase." Slide right forward, backward, or sideways followed by sliding left to meet right. First, bend both legs during the slide, and then straighten both legs while left closes to right. It can be done either with springing into the air (when legs meet and straighten) or with *releve* (without springing, when legs meet and straighten). It is similar to a gallop (like children pretending to ride a horse).

Demi plie: Standing dancer bends the knee(s) halfway, keeping heel(s) securely on the floor and torso upright.

Develope: A movement in which the working leg is first lifted, then fully extended, passing through *attitude* position. It can be done in front (*en avant*), to the side (*à la seconde*), or to the back (*derrière*).

Dorsal bend: Movement that occurs in the upper torso. It can be done by arching back, curving forward, or bending sideways.

Explode arms: Both arms shoot out from the center of the body to an upper V shape with palms facing forward, fingers stretched and apart. This action is performed quickly and with a surprising energy.

First position of arms: Position arms in front of the waist line parallel to the navel, arms are slightly curved and fingertips are pointing toward one another.

Frontal plane: Refers to the space or action occurring in the vertical plane in the front of or behind the body.

Gallop: *Chasse* with springing into the air.

Grapevine step to right: Side step right, step left across in front of right (in front of support foot), side step right, step left across behind right (behind the support foot); repeat the sequence.

Heel drag backward right: Step back right on diagonal to *demi plie*, shifting right hip out and dragging left heel on floor toward body (right hip leading the movement), left knee straight, left foot flexed. Hands in fists are placed on hips. Straight torso tilts forward with each step, head in line with torso.

Hop with wiggles: Spring into the air on both legs while stretching the legs toward the floor. Land on both legs with knees bent and feet slightly apart. Move the shoulders, alternating front and back while the arms hang down loose. Allow the arms to react freely and naturally to the shoulders moving, causing them to "wiggle" in the air.

Lunge: The leading foot is thrust forward, side or back, with the knee bent while the other leg is straightened on pique back, side, or front. The weight of the body is on the leading foot.

Parallel attitude: Attitude when working leg is not turned out.

Parallel demi plie: *Demi plie* on both legs or on one leg, feet/foot pointed straight ahead. If on both legs, can be done either with legs together or apart.

Parallel passe: *Passe* forward when working leg is pointed straight ahead (not turned out).

Pas de basque to right: Start in *demi plie* on left, with right leg bent in front, right toes touching floor. Circle right toes on the floor to right, and do small leap onto right foot, turning head slightly to right. Cross left in front of right on *releve*, shifting weight onto left then back to right into *demi plie*.

Passe: Standing on supporting leg, the working leg is bent so that the thigh is horizontal and foot is placed at knee level of the supporting leg.

Pivot on right to right: Step forward right in to *demi plie*, shifting weight on it and leaving left foot in place on floor. By quickly straightening the right knee, simultaneously doing *releve* on right and *spotting*, rotate to right on the ball of right foot to the desired degree of rotation.

Pivot step on right: Maintaining left leg in the same place the whole time, step with right forward and turn 180 degrees to left. The weight is on the right leg. Switch weight of the body to the left leg, step right forward, passing beyond the left leg. Put weight on the right, and turn to the left 180 degrees. Repeat.

Prancing: Hop onto right and put weight on right foot. Simultaneously lift left knee in *parallel front attitude*, and then repeat to left. Legs are sharp and toes point as soon as they leave the floor. While prancing, torso remains straight, elbows are bent in sharp angle, elbows and upper arms touching body, forearms front, wrists bent down, and hands are hanging.

Presentational arms: Starting from first position arms, gesture the arms open to the sides in the horizontal plane with palms facing up.

Rainbow step to right: Side *step together* right with *windmill arms* to right.

Rainbow turn: Do *windmill arms* while executing a *pivot step*.

Relevé: Commonly used in ballet, *relevé* is a movement in which the dancer rises on the tips of the toes or on the balls of the feet. This movement can be performed on both legs simultaneously or on one leg (with the other foot not touching the floor).

Sagittal plane: Refers to the space or action occurring in the vertical plane on the sides of the body.

Second position (of arms): Arms out to the sides.

Second (II) position (of legs): Legs turned out and in a wider stance (wider than shoulder width apart).

Side body wave right: Standing on the left leg, the right leg is stretched to the side, toes touching the floor. Bend the left knee to *demi plie*, shift the left hip to the side so the torso bends to right. Gradually shift the weight of the body on the right leg so both legs are in *second (II) position demi plie*. Push the right hip to right side so the torso bends to left, and shift the weight onto right leg in demi plie. Straighten right knee, finishing standing on right leg with left leg stretched to the side and toes touching floor. During the whole sequence, keep the torso in the vertical plane (no movement forward or backward). This movement is performed smoothly and sequentially.

Spotting: A term given to the movement of the head and focusing of the eyes while turning. The dancer chooses a spot in front at eye level, and as the turn is made toward the spot, the head is the last to leave and the first to arrive at the spot as the body completes the turn. This rapid movement or snap of the head gives the impression that the face is always turned forward and prevents the dancer from becoming dizzy.

Step together with right: Step right to side, or forward or backward, and close left leg to right leg.

Support leg or standing leg: The leg on which full body weight is being supported.

Waltz step: This is a traveling step based on three counts:

    Count 1: Slide right leg forward, bending both knees. Put weight on right leg.

    Count 2: Step left front passing right leg. Finish standing on left in toestand, both legs straight, weight on left.

    Count 3: Repeat count 2 to opposite side.

Windmill arms right: Starting with both arms down on left side of body, torso turned to left, right arm leads in *frontal plane*, reaching high and to the right side. Left follows in same plane. Finish with both arms down on right side of body, torso turned to right. Head/focus follows arm movements.

Conclusion

Having completed these group dances is quite an accomplishment—and a healthy one at that. Congratulations! Dancing with others requires careful coordination and close listening to the music at the same time as you are having fun. Now, if you are up to the challenge, venture into our second book, *Dancing for Fun, Book Two*. You will be dancing again, and you will have even more fun.

Links To Dances

Dance Title	Link to YouTube
Dance 1 – "Riverflow"	http://youtu.be/A87PJ3ofKpl?list=PLMXzOm_ewb6lpLvd PcbiGTP-dxottjGlJ
Dance 2 – "Spring Rain"	http://youtu.be/qoCX7kasZ2s?list=PLMXzOm_ewb6lpLvd PcbiGTP-dxottjGlJ
Dance 3 – "Just Gettin' By"	http://youtu.be/VEFqYQcv-qY?list=PLMXzOm_ewb6lpLvd PcbiGTP-dxottjGlJ
Dance 4 – "Soul Song"	http://youtu.be/841lToBWXqw?list=PLMXzOm_ewb6lpLvd PcbiGTP-dxottjGlJ
Dance 5 – "Rainbow"	http://youtu.be/JYEkS7oywAo?list=PLMXzOm_ewb6lpLvd PcbiGTP-dxottjGlJ
Dance 6 – "Fall Calypso"	http://youtu.be/X2gvyjsoQqw?list=PLMXzOm_ewb6lpLvd PcbiGTP-dxottjGlJ
Dance 7 – "Mourek Saunter"	http://youtu.be/_czE9DVJIHY?list=PLMXzOm_ewb6lpLvd PcbiGTP-dxottjGlJ
Dance 8 – "Macek Rag"	http://youtu.be/gs8GrqhrO8Y?list=PLMXzOm_ewb6lpLvd PcbiGTP-dxottjGlJ
Dance 9 – "Awakening"	http://youtu.be/PDsVbBfKaYc?list=PLMXzOm_ewb6lpLvd PcbiGTP-dxottjGlJ

Dance 10 – "Stepping Along"	http://youtu.be/7nCZzdNdVmc?list=PLMXzOm_ewb6lpLvd PcbiGTP-dxottjGlJ
Dance 11 – "Waltz in Eb"	http://youtu.be/cMK9GgMT2PA?list=PLMXzOm_ewb6lpLvd PcbiGTP-dxottjGlJ
Dance 12 – "Scrambling"	http://youtu.be/wqdqColh3QQ?list=PLMXzOm_ewb6lpLvd PcbiGTP-dxottjGlJ